FROM MY WINDOW
By Marjolein Bastin

WRITTEN AND ILLUSTRATED BY
Marjolein Bastin

STYLED BY
Charlie Mackaman

EDITED BY
Gary Higgins

Manufactured for and © 1994 Hallmark Cards, Inc.
Kansas City, MO 64141

Printed in China

FROM MY WINDOW
By Marjolein Bastin

I've always been fascinated by birds. One of my first serious nature drawings was of a finch, and I gave it to my father as a birthday present. I remember that drawing very clearly. I drew a nice apple blossom branch underneath him so he could stand... and I also gave him a bright house! He looked very happy to me. I was so proud.

Today I find birds just as exciting and delightful. As I look from my window, I see them doing so many things, and they are curious about everything! Each one seems to have its own personality. I know so many of them and am just as aware of newcomers as I am of old friends. I enjoy their visits so much.

Right next to my studio hangs a birdhouse. And it's never boring. It is full of activity all day long. The current residents have made it "cozy" with mosses and grasses lining their nests with what they think will make a delightful home. With huge energy and great enthusiasm, they will search and discover all sorts of things... all the bits and pieces that they like. Small twigs of evergreen...

whiskers from a rabbit... thin blades of grass...
even hairs from Skotta, my Iceland pony.

And just like them, I, too, cannot resist the
wonders around me. When I see something,
I think, "Oh, this is wonderful," and I can
hardly wait to pick up my pencils and brushes.
I want to draw it immediately, and I want
people to feel my excitement through my drawings.
A stonechat family waiting their turn at an
old birdbath... eggs bluer than the bluest sky... a nest full of hungry
babies. So many things too wonderful to resist.

Birds add so much to our lives. They are so happy and so expressive.
I hope you enjoy this little peek into the sights which are such a part
of my world. I want to share my drawings and thoughts with the
hope that they will touch you as much as my bird friends have
touched me.

Oh, if there were
only more time to just
stare outside a little
in the direction
of the bird feeder.
That way, you get
to know the birds better.
There's so much to see...
and I'm so easily distracted.
Birds are so woven
into my work.

A variety of bird feeders provides many kinds of outdoor dining.

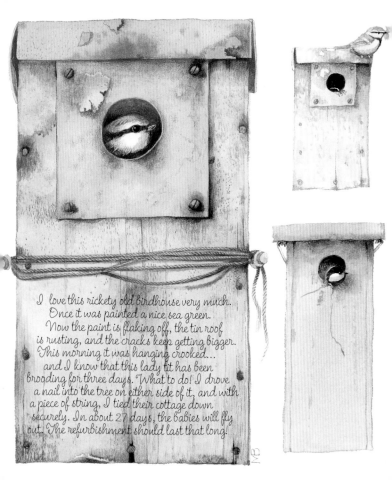

I love this rickety old birdhouse very much.
Once it was painted a nice sea green.
Now the paint is flaking off, the tin roof
is rusting, and the cracks keep getting bigger.
This morning it was hanging crooked...
and I know that this lady tit has been
brooding for three days. What to do! I drove
a nail into the tree on either side of it, and with
a piece of string, I tied their cottage down
securely. In about 27 days, the babies will fly
out. The refurbishment should last that long!

MB

My birdhouses are filling
up so nicely!

This birdhouse
has just been
occupied by
wrens.

The female nuthatch
goes inside with shreds
of bark.

The coal tit sits
under the pergola.

The blue tits enjoy
the little birch trunk
under the gutter.

I received this nice
house as a gift.

It's always a wonder to discover nests.
The most beautiful nest that I ever found is this finch nest.
It's so delicate, made with so much love, so complete.

I have great admiration for the birds who build sturdy nests
on such shaky branches! They use many kinds of materials...
twigs, stalks, straw, moss, feather, fluff, hair or wool.
And every nest is unique!

Goldfinch

Whinchat

Hedge Sparrow

Stonechat

Bullfinch

European Robin

Have you ever seen anything so wonderful?

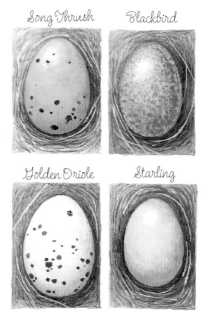

Song Thrush   Blackbird

Golden Oriole   Starling

Each egg is different and has markings as individual
as a thumbprint. And each is so beautiful
in its own way. Individual masterpieces, really.

Willow Warbler

Hedge Sparrow

European Robin

Redstart

Wren

Pied Flycatcher

Finch

Whinchat

Tree Sparrow

Lark

Titmouse

Reed Bunting

hoo-weet

Ah, what's this I hear? A stretched-out "hoo-weet, weet" and then sounds of coots, alternated with bits of starling. Then the teasing whistle again. It seems as though there are ten kinds of birds singing in the treetop, each one from a different branch, and they never get tired! But there is only one bird! It's an icterine warbler, and he can perfectly mimic many other kinds of birds. He is quite convincing! When he sings, he enthusiastically opens his beak as wide as he can so you can see his bright orange throat...

Like father, like son. Bright orange throats. You just have to learn to sing out, little ones!

What's this?
Two young robins on
the faucet in the vegetable
garden! That happens
when you're away.
I don't even know when
they were born!

The apple trees already have apples on them. But there are almost no apples which haven't been picked at. But the birds that eat them are so beautiful that I can't deny them an apple treat!

It won't be long until a family of bluebirds occupy their new home.

The bluebirds have
found a birch tree that
will make a nice home
to raise their young ones.
The female flies
in and out a few times
and decides that it will
do nicely.

The male starts building
the nest pronto!

It's always
dinnertime
according to the
young bluebirds.

This wagtail takes advantage of the fence post to use as a stage.
The dairy cows seem to enjoy the impromptu concert!

For my birthday,
I got a magnificent
hawk- and fox-proof
chicken feeder.
A chicken castle
of sorts...
right by my workroom.

I couldn't be
any happier...
I have chicks
again!
There are ten,
actually,
and two roosters.
Chatter and
laughter
are always
at the
chicken house
now.

All birds have one thing in common when it comes to feeding time-

filling hungry stomachs!

Do you suppose the hummingbird knows how beautifully he matches the fuchsias? What a perfect combination!

Swans... in love... engaged... married.

Swans "marry" for life. They are very romantic to each other and very loyal and protective of their family.

Even in the heart of a great city you can find nature. This stone birdbath in New York City's Central Park seems to be a favorite of the blue jays.

Along the high-water line there are hundreds of washed-up feathers--from scoters, eider ducks, and shelducks.

Sleepy oyster catchers on the beach near our summer house hop a few yards farther along as we walk past them. Some don't even bother to pull their heads out of their feathers!

See how beautiful they are once they're dry and clean of sand and salt!

Two stock doves
billing and cooing.

WILLEMSPAD.

A meadow pipit on a very strange post.

And this redshank
picked the most beautiful
post of all.
He must have been
looking for something
that matched
his orange legs!

Wouldn't you
come up short
just this much barbed wire...
but farmers always
find a way.

Waxwings always wear such a dramatic mask!

Goldfinches don't care how beautiful the sunflower is... they just find it delicious. They come to dine in small groups and often bring their children with them. They casually "do" the sunflowers.

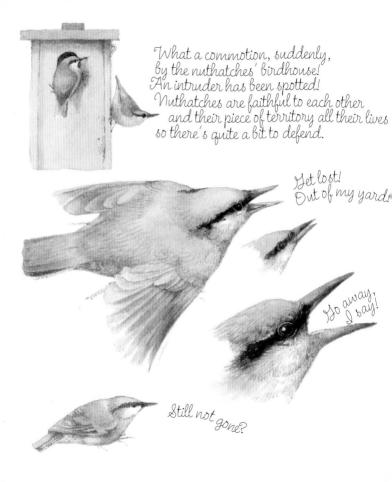

What a commotion, suddenly,
by the nuthatches' birdhouse!
An intruder has been spotted!
Nuthatches are faithful to each other
and their piece of territory all their lives
so there's quite a bit to defend.

Get lost!
Out of my yard!

Go away,
I say!

Still not gone?

Look who is perching among these wonderful wildflowers... I couldn't ask for a more beautiful subject to paint!

This robin has found a nice fence to take a little rest.

There is almost no more water in the old birdbath under the gorse bush. I can tell from the stonechat... he's sitting all the way on the bottom and there are no drops of water flying around.

Quickly, I must fill it from the blue teakettle.

Immediately, a stonechat father arrives with his two children. One of them is still so hungry that he opens his beak wide, even while bathing!

But Pa just wants to take a bath now

Bathing is so contagious that soon Ma Stonechat
and the other children have joined the group.

Is it surprising that I can't pay complete attention to my work?

Wrens will nest everywhere-- in woodpiles, bushes, and even in vegetation on the ground. But this wren is very smart. In the old greenhouse near the vegetable garden is where he's investigating to make a home. On the shelves we keep empty flowerpots, and they just might be the perfect place to raise a family.

There are plenty of tools that look unused that make handy perches.

Being close to the vegetable garden makes it easier to find tasty earthworms and nesting materials. Who needs a fancy home as long as you are in love?

We take an afternoon off to sweep the driveway
and clean up the blown-down branches.
But even this dreary work
has been delightfully interrupted.
A European robin stops by
for a quick visit. But then he flies away.

And now he's back again!

He sits on the broom, right next to me.
He looks at me... looks away...
looks at me again...
Then he sings--very softly,
very carefully.
The red feathers on his neck vibrate
to the sweet sound of his music...
The door to paradise is ajar
for a moment..